Adam Horovitz

Slow Migrations

Indigo Dreams Publishing

First Edition: Slow Migrations
First published in Great Britain in 2025 by:
Indigo Dreams Publishing
24, Forest Houses
Cookworthy Moor
Halwill
Beaworthy
Devon
EX21 5UU

www.indigodreamspublishing.com

Adam Horovitz has asserted his right under the Copyright, Designs and Patents Act 1988 to be identified as the author of this work.

ISBN 978-1-912876-94-5

British Library Cataloguing in Publication Data. A CIP record for this book can be obtained from the British Library.

Designed and typeset in Palatino Linotype by Indigo Dreams.
Cover image © Copyright Cotswold District Council, Courtesy of Corinium Museum, used with permission:
www.coriniummuseum.org.
Printed and bound in Great Britain by 4edge Ltd.

Papers used by Indigo Dreams are recyclable products made from wood grown in sustainable forests following the guidance of the Forest Stewardship Council.

for Caroline Molloy

Acknowledgements

This book would not have been possible without Chris Cundy, who commissioned me to write poems to embed into his musical responses to the exhibits at Corinium Museum and The Roman baths at Bath for his Resonance FM documentary series *Archaeology of the Ear*.

I was very glad, too, for the company of artist Dominyka Vinčaitė, sound engineer Şafak Ekmen and all the musicians who played Chris's scores and aided his improvisations - their artistic and practical input into the research process, and the sound and shape of these poems, was invaluable.

Thanks are due to Caroline Morris, Katharine Walker, Emma Stuart, James Harris and Sarah Lewis from Corinium Museum, Amanda Hart and Zosia Matyjaszkiewicz from the Roman baths in Bath, and Emma Laws from Exeter Cathedral Library, for allowing time and access to exhibits and storage facilities, and for explaining in exhilarating detail anything that needed explaining.

Thanks also to the staff and students at University of Plymouth School of Biomedical Sciences, Lee Hutt, Enus Fina, Iga Wieczorek, and Ioanna Giannakidou for their vivid explanations of water-based microorganisms and nematode worms, and to the late Professor Tim Darvill, whose strict instructions to not make too many assumptions when writing about archaeology I mostly obeyed.

Thanks also to Katy Evans-Bush for casting her sharp editorial eye over the manuscript and to Zaffar Kunial for permission to quote his poem Snowdrops, which appears in England's Glory (Faber, 2022).

A version of Water, Prayer previously appeared in *Lung Jazz*, published by Cinnamon Press. All the poems included here, except The Old Roads and Roadside Manifestos, were broadcast on Resonance FM as part of Chris Cundy's *Archaeology of the Ear* documentary series.

CONTENTS

FOREWORD by Amanda Hart

Museums are places of delight and fascination. Housing the material remains of past cultures, they promote a sense of intrigue about how our ancestors once lived. One object can hold multiple interpretations and create a different emotional response depending on the person experiencing it. Museums have become places of co-creation, actively seeking participation in storytelling, to reveal new insights and narratives. This is precisely what Adam's *Slow Migrations* does.

Slow Migrations is a collection of poems inspired by the Neolithic and Bronze Age archaeology of the Cotswolds on display at the Corinium Museum, Cirencester, and the prehistoric and Roman artefacts from the Roman bathing and temple complex, and Sacred Spring located at the heart of the iconic Roman Baths, Bath. This book is the culmination of the creative projects *The Archaeology of the Ear* and *A Sound Map of the Roman Baths,* both generously funded by Arts Council England and Help the Musicians Fund. The projects were an artistic collaboration with the renowned musician Chris Cundy, who composed the soundscapes, filmmaker Dominyka Vinčaitė, and Adam who wrote the poems.

Through his evocation of lost landscapes, people, animals and ancient objects, Adam reimagines the past with vivid detail, weaving in myths and science, descriptions you would not encounter on a museum label. Archaeology is a process, excavation and display are part of it, touched upon in *Inspecting the Curses,* but the long-term care and research of collections kept in museum stores is also a core purpose of the museum, beautifully highlighted in *Unboxing the Dead.*

Adam's thoughtfully crafted poems, drawing on recent curation and research, are a testimony to the important role museums play and the wonderful possibilities for new interpretations.

Amanda Hart
Director of Art and Archaeology, Roman Baths Museum

Slow Migrations

The Old Roads

Neolithic & Bronze Age Gloucestershire

"The dead remember. Who said that?
I said that, said the dead."

from 'Snowdrop' by Zaffar Kunial

Old Roads

We walk on old roads,
ones we've always walked.
In these days of safety we're
more prone to talk than trade.

> Look back six thousand years.
> There's a hunter with his dogs.
> *Six moons now on the move.*
> *The boar have run us hard.*

Hounds growl at nearby trees.
Stone spear raised, he sprints
slant into the woods as if carried
by the baying echo of the pack.

*

Three thousand years back now.
The woodland's sparse. Farms
are pocked with scars of cultures past.
There are strangers on the road.

> At fortified gates, they call:
> *A long journey we've had of it*
> *walking north out of the spring.*
> *We have ore to trade, and skills.*

They're welcomed in. Things move
as they always have. The world
expands and shifts. New travellers
bring new gods; now and then they stay.

A Place in the River

The human story is cyclical
as water. It changes boundaries,

evaporates, comes back as rain,
falls in unexpected places,

rushes through everything
unstoppable as a river.

So much is changed by it. Made
myth beneath water-turned earth.

> What is needed of myth is truth
> and, out of truth, fact.
>
> Of fact, we require a narrative
> that leads us to a history
>
> so that from that history we
> can make stories, deep truths
>
> that are reasonable enough
> to explain a mythic world.

Work carefully with earth and water.
Let it run through your hands

as if they were sieves, delicate
instruments for divining particles

of things unforeseen. Each tiny
piece of the past, right down to dust,

has a meaning. A place in the river.
In the endless course of us.

Slow Migration

Stone was a migrant too. Explored desire lines
in hand and sack and cart, as hammer or axe,
until at last it dropped into deep confines
of river mud from weary travellers' packs

when wars were lost or traders died
with stone in hand. A slow migration. A boast
of home, its colours carried for the long ride,
fitted to human hands, from coast to coast.

Stone travelled far, as all technology must.
Swarmed to places where the need for flint
and obsidian was great. People traded trust;
stone just journeyed. Fell and left its print.

Erosion takes time. Stone's nomadic lode
speaks across centuries in demotic code.

Axe Head from the River

i
Follow the Churn back to its source
through a matrix of reservoirs and quarries

to where the flint axe was found, spackled
with the river pigments of millennia

rust orange, moss green

buried deep in the muck of life,
trodden in by a billion footsteps. A river

reveals all in time. God-gifts sit huggermugger
in the mud with forgotten things, lost treasures

fragmentary, confused.

Water washes away centuries, blasts
history's sediment into new configurations.

People dig into these revealed histories.
Collect, collate. Assemble the past like a jigsaw

of time and space and loss.

ii

To pin carved stone down to its exact
moment of creation is tricky. A game,
at best, of inspired guesswork
          plus a process of detection.
Seek out what lay in earth with stone.
What bones clasped stone. Determine
the genus of seed scattered in stone's wake.

Round up the years, or round them down
to the nearest epoch that makes sense.
It's flint. An axe. Carved in such a way
          as to suggest, say, 40,000 years
have passed since someone knapped it sharp,
cut antlers from deer, chopped branches
for the fire, fought wolves or other men.

No picture can be perfect at such distance.
The past is a swarm of pixels, a preserved
blur of unrecorded eons, its innocence and pain
          marked out in stone.
This axe, even at forty millennia's remove,
is a flash of clarity in the slow-built
fossil image of mankind's frailty and need.

iii

A fist of flint. A sharp heart
            heavy in my hand.
It's only a replica, the curator says,
but even so the centuries weigh
hard on untested modern arms.

I stroke its edges with cautious fingers.
            Yes, this could cut
or even kill. No quick death though.
This is not a tool for hunters
who honour and respect their prey.

Back into the box it goes, this anaemic,
            un-rivered shadow
of a more desperate age. The real axe
hangs behind glass, its blaze contained.
Stone calls across history from its cage.

Earth-bound, Wind-bound
at Hazleton North long barrow

Earth binds the bones
beneath your feet.
Pig skull, cow skull,
human femur.
Like words on a page
they lie under grass,
ready for the world
to reclaim lost voices,
remember what was said.

Move out of the dark,
away from cold shadows
onto the bright hilltop.
The world opens
beneath you like a river
to windrush, scribbled
horizon line, the endless
light of a morning
sheared from its place in time.

In the deep folds of the land
time moves through soil
like worms, reducing matter
down to aerated basics.
Bonescape, stoneyard,
book to be read by gentle hands.
On this high hill, histories whisper.
Build into a story that waits,
wind-bound, for willing ears.

The Flint Knapper

In the long barrow's doorway
a man clutches his tools just so,
as if he could still knap flint
in whatever place his people believed
lay beyond the world we think we know.

Articulated in death as he was in life
his positioning speaks of unpicked
codes laid at knowledge's border,
boundaries of belief. He is a way-marker
for ways forgotten and unknown.

So much has been lost, yet the puzzle
remains intact, stripped of meat and muscle
till what's left is this skeletal puppet
resurrected from the intimacy of soil. See here,
the traces of someone consumed by stone.

Beyond him, in the barrow, a rune-scatter
of assorted bones. Guard at the path
to death, or life. He is a message
lost in translation, time-swallowed.
Left at the tipping point of change.

Unboxing the Dead

Man as jigsaw
kept in cardboard box
each bone in plastic bags
scapula almost connected
to humerus, mandible, fibula.

      A glossary scattered in storage.

Dirt and dig-dust
housed in separate boxes
await technology's advances.
All will be useful one day
to claim the truths of bone

      from myth or expectation.

Let this man remain uncoloured
by the sympathy of naming.
Leave that for children
who wrap all they encounter
in flesh or clothes,

      wind everything into a story.

For now, we must learn
what we can in the hard light
of this climate controlled room.
Contain the bone-dance. Mute
the thrill of trying too hard

      to imagine lives unlike our own.

Beneath the Barrow

Under the soil, a barrow.
Under the barrow, a longhouse.
Throughout the longhouse, lines of memory
traced in stone, wood and bone fragment.
Lineage and loves laid out
in lengthened spirals through the earth
under shelves of rock. A family's world
compressed into lost acreage,
into the deep marrow of lives lived
                and farms tended.

The long dead have all but worn away,
their daily truths and compromises
consumed by a never-ending squall
of water, air and time; by a sinuous
coil of roots. All that breaks life down
into its component parts.
Yet they are not lost entirely.
People live on in splinters,
in a scrawled graffiti of genetics
that only fire can utterly consume.

So, under the barrow, a longhouse.
Throughout the longhouse
a puzzle-board of possibilities
that give up secrets to patient hands
and careful eyes. Yes, humans lived here once.
Died here, and were celebrated.
Post holes remain to mark their plasticity
in traces of a house beneath a cairn
where history mulches down with myth
and facts wait to grow like dormant seed.

An Early History of Money

In the long days before money,
we traded need for need,
the song of want
bound to our tongues
with subtle harmonies.
Have this, if it will serve you.
Make fire / axes / dig your stone.
A measure of food?
> *Yes, and shelter.*
> *Two nights at least*
> *before we travel on.*

Then came bronze.
From alchemy, commodity
scoured from the deep earth.
Pretty grave goods,
godheads, weapons,
decorations for the hearth,
for structures that settle
into homes. New forms
rose from its smelting.
Bronze travelled, mixed
till all trace of its origin was lost.

Iron next. Found everywhere.
A weaker weapon but an easy trade.
Kept in sword-length strips,
metal cut to the required size
for weights of grain.
Worth divisible, of use
to all people. Unlike coins;
gold and silver was for chieftains,
ritually exchanged for passage
across land, through markets.
A border stamped with a king's face.

Horse/Power

White horse carved
   on the horizon
as guide and totem.
   Signal for travellers.
In their pockets, coins
   stamped with echoes of a horse.

Way-marker for the well-worn
   track connecting tribes
in straight lines above difficult terrain
   to places of commerce
where people met and symbols
   changed their dress.
Took on aspects of the tribes'
   deep-rooted needs, desires.

This is how money arrives.
   Pressed into the heads of men
in need of a common tongue,
   who press ideas out
into silver, gold. A Macedonian horse
   made strange by new eyes,
the limits of a carver's skill.
   Imagination trapped in metal.

What do you know of horses?
  That they are wealth.
Power rests on the back of them.
  The old trade roads are long.
Printed deep with hoof-marks
  and human movement.

What we recognise as money
  began with horses, travelled
with horses, echoed in the hills
  of many countries, cantered
in the wake of Philip of Macedon
  across countless borders.

Take the idea of horse
  and change it by increment.
A charioteer's hand shifts
  into a crescent moon.
Armour becomes eye. Tails
  are triplicated. Horses
real and unreal proliferate
  to suit tribal visions.
It is all money. All horse.
  Power rests in pockets.
Before long, the horse
  learns how to ride the man.

The Thread
at Bagendon, Gloucestershire

> "The village is, in miniature,
> what the world is, near or far"
> *from 'The Village' by Frank Mansell*

i

Mycelial threads of history
run beneath scattered cottages,
through the bones of the church.
Under the farmland's skin,
thickened by centuries,
the old world remembers itself.

A walker on a quiet lane,
blinkered by hedgerows, may not see
time's long, threaded networks, only:
*there, a plough-turned coin; a raised
fist of grass and stone on the horizon.*
The masked industries of the dead

ride through the soil unsung.
Tribes shift like seasons over millennia
transient as autumn leaves,
but their tools remain, their architectures.
Somewhere in the earth, a code, unbroken
till we learn the proper ways to dig.

ii

Four phases of industry beneath
bucolic skin; a tribe's capital
lost to the sweep of empire.
Smelting furnace. Blowing pits.
The royal mint of the Dobunni.

Iron and bronze brooches,
carpenter's hobnails,
probable coin dies.
Spring tongs, steel wire,
ox goad, gouge.
Awls and other tools,
A knife, a door-latch.
Timber cramps.

Land shaped by the deep histories
of horse tamers, warriors and smiths;
by our actions and theirs. Their toil,
occluded, sings on in the unwritten
harmonies of continuous human life.

Bronze pendants from a necklace,
parts of a squared mirror,
ornamental fittings.
Fish-hook. Elongated
lead pellets, hook attachments.
Slingstones. Fragments of crucible.
Coin mould. An intensely heated daub.
Glass fragments. Pots.

Tools evolve into money, money
into swords, swords into ploughshares.
In this village that was once a city
thread speaks to thread through
a soil record of unceasing work.

The Shape of Your Hands
i.m. Ed Watkins

Clay at the river's edge,
toad-mottled by leaf light
as it glances from water.

It sings from the reed banks;
climb down to it, hand
over hand. Scoop up a ragged ball

to turn and mold, then
press your thumbs in deep.
Pinch at the slippery mass

until lump gives way
to vessel. A shape that fits
the contour of your hands

as they are cupped to drink.
Pinch on until walls thin
to the point where heat

will transfer without scalding,
hold broth but not break.
Shaping's such a human instinct.

*

You are with your ancestors now
in the slippage point between times,
doing what they did, learning

as you go. Difference slips away
like water. This clay is as much
the clay they pulled from river banks

as any clay. It sits brown and heavy
in your hand as it ever sat in theirs.
A weight like hope. The river

runs god-like as all thought
through the possibilities of making.
Find a fire for your pot and bake it.

Pray that, in six thousand years, someone
will be astonished by your fingerprints.
By the steadfast shape of your hands.

Microlith Music
at Corinium Museum

These are the teeth we pulled
from the jaws of the past;
a handful of pinned notes,
their shadows cast as piano sharps
and flats on a museum wall.

> Behold: twenty-two
> segments of suspended time.

Once, they were tools for survival,
for making and undoing.
Keys to a life run hard
beneath looping symphonies
of sun's rise, season's shift.

Now, a long diminuendo
of light and blood lingers
in each arrow- and spear-head,
each vicious harpoon barb
caught in soft-spun light.

> Behind glass, each slivered note
> of this fossilised music resonates

with a song of *life-in-death, death-in-life*.
A cappella only, but still ready for an aria.
For orchestras of wood and leather to bind
these barbs of quick despatch back in
to the brutal music of their making.

Wolf Under Glass

First follower. Scavenger.
          Slave to the hunt.
Drawn into human circles
by excarnation, meat waste,
blood frenzy, offerings of offal,
scraps of bloodied skin.

Caught in a trap of plenty.
Hunt reduced to ease.
          Glut and feast.
Wolf body broken and reformed
by close contact with a new pack.

Reduced and honed.
          Senses narrowed.
Bone and muscle bred
to be akin to arrow, spear, hammer.
A warm body built
for nights of desperate cold.

Come into the fold, puppy.
Out of the snow. Your wild days
are over before they began.
Time to be simmered, over centuries,
into loyalty, protection, warmth.

Be a follower of gestures,
obedient to the bigger pack.
Lose the determination of chase
and jaw to the tool-makers' will;
to the sound of a master's voice.

Before the farm, the dog,
marking boundaries for the hunt.
Prey fenced into killing grounds.
Monocultures of blood.

Forest made safe by dogs
for fragile men who carved
wolf flesh like stone
into their own image.

To the fluid world an order
softened by flesh and fur.
Dog and human, in symbiosis,
taming one another by degrees.

Under glass, a Bronze Age dog.
A bone-ghost of devotion laid out to honour
close-knit lives of pact and sympathy;
long arrangements built across millennia.

Marked in death for a place of privilege
in the pack. Tool and child at once,
carefully placed. Long histories of understanding
turned to tenderness. Abstracted, magnified.

Made into a story; dog and man running together.
The pack's complex hierarchies fossilised.
Codes of love exposed under refracted light.
A pattern to be read by anyone, living or long dead.

Listen to the Pigs

Listen to the pigs
as they root
in long grass
    turn up earth &
    scratch for food

Simple voices
crossing borders
all but unchanged
        a small language
        of search and succour

even as their bodies
were stretched
to meet our needs
        bones added
        genes altered

Listen to the pigs
How they speak
to us, for us,
    in familiar tones,
    of journeys

diversions, travels
through the deep
muck of history
        digging out
        our shared roots

along a common trail
following ciphered
lines of ancient fields
        a grammar of bones
        scored beneath soil

An Assumption About Animals

Bone in the barrow's forecourt.
Multiple fragments of cattle and swine
surrounding the mouth of the tomb.

Fleshy head of pig pinned to the wall.
Guide pig, psychopomp, totem. Its voice
translated in snatches by hungry crows.

In their beaks, the eyes they've plucked
flicker like beacons lit in other worlds.
A burial party comes grunting to the gates,

lingers in the shadow of the pig. The cold,
familiar rituals of loss are marked
on the floor with picked-clean bone.

The tomb laid out like a body,
a stretched hide to contain the dead.
Man and animal at one in the dark.

Bodies wrapped in bodies, bound
to the symbolism of flesh. Man and beast
rotting together as they lived, in unison.

Water, Prayer

Aquae Sulis, The Roman Baths

"If I were called in
To construct a religion
I should make use of water."

from 'Water' by Philip Larkin

Roadside Manifestos

Codes and way-markers of millennia
scattered among flowers, grasses
by passing hawkers, hoods tipped
against rain; by refugees in uncertain
weathers escaping ravaged lands.

We came this way following the river,
the setting sun. Left war behind us,
fled the warriors and their frenzy.
Came looking for a life. Walked across
waters and lands we barely understood.

Traces of soldiers, armies. Dropped
weapons. Tools. Elements of language
run like wire through new maps
...to bring hope to the lost places. An empire
of old roads straightened and made new.

Roadside gods rise up, walk off
with decurions, traders, thieves. Follow
the priests who follow the scent of change
upriver to places of community,
healing, towards the rise of sacred steam.

Centuries of men, women, children
walking the loose change of continents
– like Hansel's stones–into history's paragraphs.
We settle words onto the land like seeds
which grow into manifestos, creeds, beliefs.

The Sacred Spring at Dawn
Aquae Sulis, Bath

i
Bubble-prayers
rise in silver clusters –
         a jellyfish wriggle
         through green water –
sulphurous globes
that catch the morning
unawares. A shiver-
scent of centuries adrift
         in the city's heart.
Gas dreams of the deep
rising through a shimmer
of sky and stone
         caught like breath
         in the sacred spring –
         muted, mouthed, swallowed
         in this sacramental shift
         between states of green.

ii
Here, time is still.
Tangibly folded.
The city's now-song
no more than an echo
in sacred water.

Our voices fuse with
looped reels of bathers
projected on worn walls;
the museum's shadow-chatter
as it wakes around us.

Slick Roman slabs
carry footsteps
in their wake, as if
water is fossil
and stone flows.

iii
Before the day's warmth
reaches stone, a song of heat
rises. Folded fingers of steam
beckon as a god would beckon.

iv
Follow the light, the silence,
the aroma of history submerged.

Don't listen to the day's bright call;
dive in to the dreaming,

the warm, misted god-space
where myth and history bathe

together, rub shoulders with the rich,
the poor, half-forgotten kings

and symbolic pigs, all of them
praying for good skin, long life,

in the sacred green inkiness
of this miraculous well.

Overflow

Coppered waterfall.
        Iron lung of goddess
exhaling hard beads

        that fall, pound
fallen water to froth.
        Long rain of millennia

spilled from the hands of Sulis,
        or Bladud's cauldron. Each drop
a mineral micro-verse, an epoch

        squeezed through limestone,
mudstone, green marl
        blue lias, collapsed debris

drawn up into the spare
        light of built-up city mornings,
on into this overflow,

        this roaring culvert
slick with metal residue
        that spills river-wards,

carries prayer and sulphur,
        geology spun with myth,
over warm, worn, gilded stone.

The Waters of Sulis/Minerva
riffing on Shakespeare's Sonnet 116

Mouth a sickle sharp as laughter,
she steps into ebullient water

> her flesh a pulse of joy and caution
> as she is consumed, then raised, on limbs

stretched across the meniscus
of this bone-warm healing soup.

> Over centuries she sinks, body
> immersed, skin mingled then lost

until all that is left is her face,
spring-fixed, a ghost in the green,

> hair become vine shadows
> traced on the water. Her skin is light.

She sees all from a place of sacrifice:
curses; altars; what alteration finds;

> the change of days; the sure, slow shift
> of ever-fixed marks. Another woman/

goddess swims into her abstracted skin.
Wisdom is washed into worship,

> dissolved into a syncretic marriage.
> Two goddesses. One mystery

caught on the streaming tongues of people
come for healing, hope or reparation;

> whatever answers may be glimpsed
> in her cyclical smile, her rippled face.

Spring Pipes

This is the music
        of that which heats
ancient rain
        as it rises, rises;
a pressure melody
        to outlast stone.

                *

        hot springs underlain by rock
        more heavily fractured
        than those of adjacent areas

                shafts and tunnels

        ground saturated

                with hot water

        spring pipes

                        collapse structures
                formed over a local high point

        carboniferous limestone sealed
        beneath a thick cover of Jurassic rocks
        until the excavation of groundwater
        in the region   confined by permafrost

        warm water
        in the limestone knoll
        close enough   to the surface
        to melt permafrost
produce springs in the valley floor

fine-grained materials in cavities
      in limestone
           removed

equilibrium   the rate of flow
balanced against
                spring pipes
                spring pipes
                spring pipes

      *

Earth's ichor
     risen over aeons
a geological song
     focused in one mouth
that sings out
     as if it were a god's.

Note: the text between the asterisks is an erasure poem drawn from
two paragraphs in 'The Geology of the Hot Springs' by R.W. Gallois.

Words for the Goddess

Words cast into the water,
taken out of circulation, beyond
human use. Only the goddess should read
these ritual carvings in metal tablets;
sacrificial slivers cast into her sacred place
where desire and rage transmute
patterns of folded lead into power.

> *To Minerva the goddess Sulis*
> *I have given the thief.*
> *The thief who has stolen*
> *my hooded cloak.*
> *Whether slave or free,*
> *whether man or woman*
> *The thief is not to buy back*
> *this gift unless with their own blood.*

A multitude of voices placed
in the mouth of the goddess.
From damp caverns water
carries fury, prayer, loss
out over her tongue –
dissolved in sulphur, torn from lead.

> *May he who has stolen*
> *my brooch from me*
> *become as liquid as water.*

Everything here is given
to the goddess, kept for the goddess,
begged of the goddess. Curses
become real under her tongue,
in the sharp cave of her mouth
where thoughts are codified, fossilised,
preserved as an archaeology of want.

Forgiveness is not
to be given to her,
nor shall she sleep,
except on condition
that Euticia sells
a bushel of cloud,
a bushel of smoke.

Inspecting the Curses

Curse in a cushioned case, fragile as thought.
Lead worn, letters faded. I can almost
touch the anger of the unknown dead. Taut
words of rage. Desire hung like a small ghost

in battered metal. In the guise of gods,
we have pierced the secrets of the past.
A crude telepathy of pokes and prods,
manipulated light and raised contrast.

These cases contain fossilised records
of human want. Fragments of the common
tongue raised in anger to beg that accords
be broken divinely. Let the lawman

slip away like water, these tablets plead,
as if vengeance is justice and want, need.

Still the Goddess Will Remain

an answer to 'The Ruin', from *The Exeter Book,* incorporating phrases
from that poem

they said it was a kingly thing
            a house, a city, a place to bathe
thinking only of the men
who claimed the land as theirs

            the goddess in the water
                        was almost forgotten
            she who ghosted her divinity

through broken tiles, cracked stone
for empty, occulted centuries

                        *

if every wall dissolves into pebbles
and the remains of glad-minded

            gold-bright men are washed away
                        worn down to sand
            still the goddess will remain

she who has never left
will never leave   until these deep
            thermal springs
sink into ruin, leaving only heaps of mud

Offerings

Names shift on the road,
over centuries, as tongues
and cultures change.
Aquae Sulis, Akemanchester,
Bath - whatever name is given
still the pilgrims come
and keep on coming, to lay
diseased skins, swords, coins,
claims, offerings and words
at the hot mouth of the spring.

*

A city is not its buildings.
It is its people and waters.
Past is palimpsest.
Ribs and roots of cities
reach down to their hot,
moist origins; component
city parts pulse like organs
caught in water light,
in the steaming bubble-beat
of this sulphurous spring.

*

Gods gather at the water's
edge, invisible but present,
each one a bacterium of belief
roiling in water as gas
rises, iron oxidises, ancient
rains come singing back
into stonescape, water course,
mare's tail cloud patterns
drawn skyward by the sun.
Science intertwined with faith.

Infinity on an Agar Plate

Nematode worm under microscope
looped like ouroboros
round on itself, mouth to tail.

Coy wriggler. Hook of hope
in a skim of sacred water. Porous
symbol written in micro-braille

at feast on bacterial, cellular
chains spread out snakelike
          in search of light.

Infinity sung in a minor key;
small songs for tiny things
that will outlive humankind.

From Sacred Spring to Agar Plate

All life is here, from deep beginnings
to the very end of things.
The old truths. The mysteries. All those
known knowns and unknown knowns
scored on stone, pewter, lead.
All that is worshipped, made sacred,
clutched at by priests' hands, is written
on water. History drips through priestly fingers,
solidifies into science. Here: see microscopic
gods bathing in warm primordial soup. The bacterial
cure-alls, methane eaters. Gods in their heaven;
a well with a nematode worm.

Water, Prayer

Water, pure in its cradle-glass,
is trembling sea in miniature, where lips
beach the meniscus and then gently pass
it back; a constant recycling of sips.

Each mouthful is a moving on, a cloud
as deeply housed as dreams of rain.
In sacred pool, in tap, in cup it's flowed
from *it* to *us,* and there, and back again.

It's in the engine of this world, the flow;
water, the roaring constancy of change.
It plumps the hidden seed and makes it grow
and can, with time, bring down a mountain range.

It is itself a prayer. Hold out your hand.
Watch water rub fear down to grains of sand.

Faces in the Water

Listen! All cultures shift like water.
Old ones are overwhelmed, their ideas
cut loose. Peoples are led to slaughter,
or assimilated by the new. Their prayers

and fears are swallowed, conflated, held
in the shallow memories of victors,
like wasps in amber, single celled,
till they too are lost. Only pictures

remain, stripped of origin and context.
The modern mind holds on to icons
akin to those it sees each day. Vexed,
misunderstood tin loses out to bronze.

In these pools, rippled histories of human faces
shimmer, reflected in god masks, in mineral traces.

Tin Mask

i
he looks rather well
        for all that his
        tin face spent
two thousand years
        caught in water
        hooked into
        a drainage duct
all clatter silenced
        by the flow of millennia
        as filth crept through
        eye sockets and time
        added its own embossments
to his small features, the angle of his nose

        ii
        Flattened & forgotten
        transition face.
                Inexact memory
                drawn from the water
        away from the last lost
        gods & their silent people.
                Voices carried
                off like rain
        into the deep places
        –the pressure-memory
                of fossil time–
                where new gods
        & invasive creeds weigh down
        like granite on ancient prayers.

iii

Mask of the goddess?
A double deity, her name ablaze.
Spoken, remembered, marked
in books, deep in the annals
of water, earth and stone.

Even now she watches over us,
her head empty as a pitcher.

Tin mask? Punctuation in water.
Graffiti tagged on history's edge.
Erased, elided. Meaning & function
slippery as dream. Brow embossed
with patterns of unknowing.

He is myth made of masks beneath masks.
A small truth awaiting fact.

In the Exeter Book, the Ruin

Come with your gloves,
your deep detective sympathy

for that which is lost
to the creep of palimpsest.

Come to the book, the poem,
the riddles & primitive magics

of translation and its comrade, faith.
There are words buried here

beneath a Rorschach-blotted
keloid scar which holds

the afterimage
& aftertaste of history

burned down to guesswork.
A breath of hope in the silences

built of leaf-mould, stolen stone,
the terror of miracles to come.

> One may think of Poetry as being like Religion, a
> modified descendant of primitive Magic; it keeps
> the family characteristic of stirring wonder by
> creating from unpromising lifeless materials an
> illusion of unexpected passionate life."
>
> ~ *Robert Graves*

Somewhere in the Steam

The water holds different voices
        different tongues
in its endless recycled eddies.

> *Song of pilgrims.*
> *Mutter of locals*
> *come to address*
> *the goddess in secret.*
> *Untranslatable tablets*
> *in Roman letters.*
> *Language unknown.*

New empires rise and travel like water
        into the secret
places of the sublimated past.

> *A song of steam*
> *eavesdrops on furies*
> *both petty and violent.*
> *It billows up to hide*
> *long dead ritual,*
> *those lessons held*
> *by the language of bodies.*

No, absence of evidence is not
        evidence of absence.
We pan for metaphysical, metaphorical gold.

> *Song of scholars*
> *and archaeologists.*
> *Slow, careful,*
> *hopeful tunes*
> *that may yet blossom*
> *into understanding*
> *somewhere in the steam.*

Votive Anchoring

They put pennies in the water.
Anchored them with prayer.
Put words into the spring.
Gave the gods their share.

Votive breasts and curses.
Sword hilts, shields and tools.
A penny or a work of art.
Stern words for thieves and fools.

> Hope weighs next to nothing
> even wedded to a coin.
> Its symbols travel in the blood;
> *the past* and *now* conjoined.

Water carries everything,
all dreams and gods and joys.
Even the wriggle of despair;
ten millennia's white noise.

It's hard not to believe that
our desires can be dispersed;
that grief's soluble in water
and the river has rehearsed

dissolving passages of prayer
into the empty mouths of gods
or carrying them on down
to the sea's evening of odds.

> Go, put a penny in the water.
> You'll have anchored it in time.
> Echoed your long dead ancestors
> with a physical act of rhyme.

The Myth of the Swineherd

Bladud. Bad luck,
bad king. Blood
on his lips,
blood on his skin.

Myth of the leper,
myth of unwashed sin.
Myth of the swineherd
observing his pigs

as they wade on down
into divine hot mud.
Slip, slump and wallow
until, skin unpocked,

smooth, less sallow,
they rise, roink and rattle
off into the forest,
run back into myth.

> Bladud, bad herder, born
> to good luck, little battle,
> follows the pigs that were his
> deep into hot springs.

Bladud, bad King, loses
leperous lesions. His skin
sings as he slumps, slides
and slips into mineral mud.

Myth of the miracle,
myth of the heat
that cleanses the man
who decides to be king,

puts a stone in the ground,
a sword in the stone.
Builds a city around it.
Forges on alone.

When the truth is forgotten
pull myth out of the mud.
Rebuild round the springs
with tales, gods and blood.

Ivory Breasts

Breasts carved
from a sword's
ivory pommel.
Carved and cast
into the waters.

Rare trace
of a woman's
presence in this
place dominated
by male demands.

Even Minerva –
goddess of strategy,
intellect, healing –
even Sulis/Minerva
measures in men's favour.

What chance that
she ever noticed
this prayer for [what?
No more mastitis?
Breast cancer cure?]

All is guesswork. We glean
what we can, imagine more.
Know only this lone note
raised in sensual defiance
above man's cacophony.

Breasts carved
from a sword's
ivory pommel.
Carved and cast
into the waters.

Also by Adam Horovitz:

Turning (Headland, 2011)
A Thousand Laurie Lees (The History Press, 2014)
Only the Flame Remains (Yew Tree, 2014)
The Physic Garden (ed.) (Palewell, 2017)
The Soil Never Sleeps (Palewell, 2018)
The Soil Never Sleeps (2nd extended edition) (Palewell, 2019)
Love & Other Fairy Tales (IDP, 2021)

Indigo Dreams Publishing Ltd
24, Forest Houses
Cookworthy Moor
Halwill
Beaworthy
Devon
EX21 5UU
www.indigodreamspublishing.com